COUNTRIES IN THIS SERIES

THE SIMPLE GUIDE TO

JAPAN

CUSTOMS & ETIQUETTE

ABOUT THE AUTHOR

HELMUT MORSBACH is known internationally for his specialist
work on Japanese culture and society, especially in the field of
non-verbal communication. He currently teaches at Shiga National
University, Japan. He is also the author of *Remembering the
Hiragana* and *Japanese Phrase Book & Dictionary*.

ILLUSTRATED BY
IRENE SANDERSON

[THIRD EDITION]

THE SIMPLE GUIDE TO

JAPAN

CUSTOMS & ETIQUETTE

Helmut Morsbach

WITH A FOREWORD BY
RONALD DORE

GLOBAL BOOKS LTD

Simple Guides • Series 1
CUSTOMS & ETIQUETTE

The Simple Guide to
JAPAN
CUSTOMS & ETIQUETTE

Global Books Ltd
PO Box 219, Folkestone, Kent CT20 3LZ, England

New Edition 1994
Reprinted 1995
Third Edition 1997
Reprinted 1999

ISBN 1-86034-021-0

British Library Cataloguing in Publication Data
A CIP catalogue entry for this book
is available from the British Library.

Set in Futura 11 on 12pt by Bookman, Hayes, Mddx.
Printed in Great Britain by
Cromwell Press, Trowbridge, Wilts.

Contents

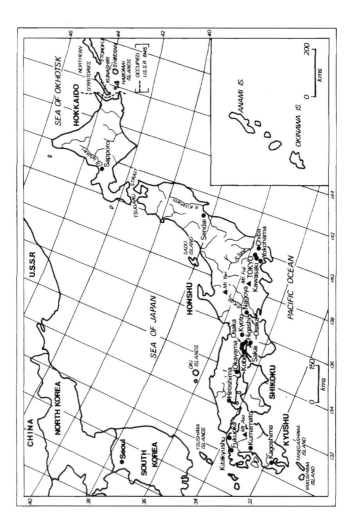

Introduction
Ronald Dore

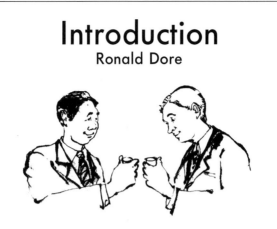

'Campai!'

Learning to do as the Tokyoites do is important when you are in Japan. Or rather, at least *trying* to do as the Tokyoites do – for the crucial thing is to demonstrate, by doing so, that one dissociates oneself from the unfortunate past and really does look forward to building relations with one's Japanese opposite numbers on the footing of mutuality, of equality of respect and consideration.

So the trying is the important thing, at least for building up *rapport*. It is a perfectly viable strategy to profess a combination of total ignorance of Japanese manners and a total willingness to be instructed. And sometimes it can even be the best strategy. Those who are trying to conform to conventions that have not become second nature can sometimes become anxious about doing the right thing, and that can introduce a tension into the relationship which actually militates against *rapport*.

Don't worry, therefore, if, when you are in mid-situation, you forget one of the wise injunctions to be found in Dr Morsbach's book. Just break off to ask your Japanese friends what is the right thing to do and they will not think the worse of you for it, because although *they* feel obliged to show familiarity with Western customs, they don't really *expect* foreigners to know theirs – because of all the history of the last hundred years.

But if you can manage *not* to forget Helmut Morsbach's advice, so much the better. He has spent a long time asking people what should properly be done in all kinds of situations, and gives an excellent summary of what one might call the etiquette of consciousness

But he also gives more than that. As a shrewd observer of the behaviour of Japanese and other peoples he has noticed some of the characteristically Japanese ways of behaving which the Japanese will *not* tell you about because they tend to take them for granted, to think of them as part of human nature and not particularly a matter of 'doing as the Tokyoites do'. His special interest is in all those ways people have of communicating without words.

Since visitors to Japan who are not going to spend years learning the Japanese language before they go may find verbal communication restricted on occasion, Helmut Morsbach's shrewd observations on gesture language should be particularly useful.

Even someone like me who has been an occasional visitor to Japan for the last 40+ years can profit from Dr Morsbach's book – partly from enjoying the accuracy of his observations, but not least from the reassurance that come from discovering that one has been getting some things wrong for 40 years, but in spite of that can still keep one's Japanese friends!

R. D.

Foreword

In Japan, traditional etiquette continues to be extremely important, even in the 1990s, despite whatever outward appearances of 'Westernization' the visitor may experience.

When arriving on business, for example, you will automatically be accorded a relatively high status, and experience polite treatment by those who matter.

Most Japanese expect that as a foreigner you will behave according to Western rules and conditioning. However, they can always be forgiven for hoping that at some point you will at least try to understand their ways.

This book, therefore, is an attempt to highlight some of the key facets of Japanese etiquette and customs that can, I hope, be committed to memory and grasped intellectually before letting experience and instinct take their course.

Although addressed principally to the person visiting Japan on business, this guide will, I hope, help 'prepare the ground' for all those who have the opportunity to discover this remarkable culture and its people.

While many other aspects (such as technology) have changed in Japan over the years, in my opinion customs and etiquette show remarkably little variation. As I prepare this Third Edition, the reader should be reassured that there is still the overriding emphasis on traditional etiquette which enables most Japanese to live harmoniously together in a crowded country. Occasional newspaper reports about crimes and disasters simply show how relatively rare these tend to be when compared to Western countries. Daily life continues in a well-regulated, predictable way.

Often, Japanese society seems to be an extremely well-functioning machine as long as no drastically new situations (e.g. the Sarin gas attacks or the Kobe Earthquake) arise. And it is in such predictable situations that correct etiquette provides much of the 'lubricant', allowing social interaction to run smoothly.

Helmut Morsbach
Spring 1997

ACKNOWLEDGEMENTS

Several friends read the various drafts and made useful suggestions; especially my publisher, Paul Norbury, and Donald Richie, as well as Professor Ronald Dore.

Naturally, I have profited from reading many books on Japan, most of all from the thorough (but sometimes outdated) *Japanese Etiquette – an Introduction*, published in 1955 by the Tokyo YWCA.

1

In General

Japanese etiquette emphasizes courteous behaviour among members belonging to a certain group. If you are properly introduced to such a group, courtesies will be shown to you as well. How should you behave, since the degree of courtesy is generally much higher than in your own culture?

Naturally, it is not expected that you know all about (or even use) the intricate Japanese ways of behaviour, and you would certainly be considered strange if you did. Instead, try to be more polite than at home, since you will be making many *faux pas* whatever you do.

Effusive thanks for minor matters are common in Japan. Therefore, try to express your own gratitude more often than at home. For instance, remember to say, 'Thank you for your kindness the other day' on meeting again (see p.68 for translation), even if this 'kindness' was so general that you would not normally have bothered referring to it.

Japanese still prefer bowing to each other on being introduced. To you, however, they will offer their hand, and will probably attempt a combination of handshake and slight bow.

Don't grip the hand too tightly, and don't expect a 'strong' handshake in return. If no hand is offered, imitate the bow you receive as regards depth and frequency. Keep your arms straight and let the palms slide down your thighs while lowering your torso.

On greeting, or during conversation, don't insist on too much eye contact – this tends to be avoided and may be regarded as impolite. Downward glances and limp handshakes should not be interpreted as 'shiftiness' or a sign of a 'weak character'.

Smiling may be a way of hiding embarrassment. Don't take it to mean assent all the time. Most Japanese turn up the corners of their mouth when speaking their own language, and thus seem to be engaged in happy banter more than they really are. Genuine happiness is indicated more accurately by creases in the corners of the eye.

Don't point to persons or objects with your index finger – this is rude. Draw attention by using the whole hand, palm turned upwards, in a flowing (not pointing) movement.

Don't express affection in public, except to small children. Avoid slapping backs or holding others by the arm while talking, except perhaps during convivial all-male drinking sessions.

Japanese generally keep a greater distance from each other when talking. Although you might feel uncomfortable and remote, don't move too close.

Loud sniffing/snuffling during a cold is not regarded as bad manners, but blowing your nose in front of others is.

Some Western gestures are generally unknown in Japan and may be misunderstood. e.g. winking, or shrugging your shoulders.

> **Top Tip**
>
> Become sensitive to vague, indirect cues asking you to do something, e.g. to get you to leave, someone might remark, 'The car is waiting.'

Most Japanese treat money like Westerners treat sex – discreetly, even 'shamefully'. There are times in a business context when for services rendered you might be handed money in an envelope and be asked to sign a receipt. To open the envelope indicates lack of trust. If it does contain less money than stated, it might be due to tax having been deducted at source. The change given in stores is usually presented on a plastic dish. It need not be counted to see if it is correct, since to be short-changed is rare. In Japan, despite many bribery scandals in government and big business, there is a great deal of honesty in everyday transactions.

Haggling over prices is usually not done, either, although a degree of 'negotiating' especially in duty-free shops, is not unknown. If you want to make money gifts, special money gift envelopes can be obtained from stationery shops. Banknotes used as gifts should not be creased (ideally mint) and can be obtained at special counters in banks.

TIPPING

You are not required to tip anybody! In fact, to do so could be regarded as insulting. One of the few exceptions may be the case when you ask a taxi driver to get out of the driver's seat so as to help you with heavy luggage in and out of the car. In such a case, you can round up the fare to the nearest thousand yen. Furthermore, in the more expensive restaurants serving Western food, waiters will not refuse a tip, but it is still not mandatory to give anything extra.

Top Tip

Exclamations of *Hai, hai* do not signal agreement (as your dictionary may tell you); rather, they indicate that the person you are talking to is still listening. Therefore try to exchange something in writing concerning any major decisions, such as exact time and location of a meeting.

'Daruma' deliberations

In a culture where males precede females, Western males may embarrass a lady if they open a door for her, or offer her a seat. This may imply that she is physically weak. Getting in and out of narrow doors (e.g. lifts) can be a problem if both hold back. Some hilarious collisions have occurred this way!

Western businesswomen on their own in Japan might find it easiest to act as they would in the West as regards precedence, etc., but not feel offended on those occasions when this is not accorded to them.

Toilet facilities for males and females are some-times unsegregated. A poker face at the urinal helps when ladies suddenly walk past behind you. Even high-class hotels may have wash-rooms without any facilities for drying ones hands. Japanese tend to use their own handkerchief for this purpose.

. . . at odds with 'polite behaviour'

While being cocooned by the attentiveness of your hosts and the hotel staff looking after you in Japan, you may at times also witness scenes at odds with 'polite behaviour'. Commuters on trains and buses face this daily during rush-hour. Pushing and overcrowding are endured silently. Dozing off while being wedged in somewhere is one way to cope. Once away from the in-group, behaviour can change drastically.

With its complex and colourful history and culture Japan is a fascinating topic to read about. It is well worth the trouble reading as widely as you can before leaving. In Japan, all the major hotels stock considerable quantities of English-language books and journals.

Japanese bookshops with special departments for Western books on Japan include some shops of the Maruzen chain (e.g. central Tokyo and Kyoto), the Kinokuniya chain (e.g. Shinjuku and Sibuya areas of Tokyo as well as Umeda Station of the Hankyū Railway in Osaka), the Jena bookstore in the Tokyo Ginza area, the Byblos bookshop in Tokyo's Takada-no-Baba area, and the Avanti bookshop near Kyoto station.

For their exact locations (as well as other tourist information about Japan), you can make use of the 'Travel-Phone' service, operated by the Tourist Information Centre (TIC). Their Tokyo number is 03–3503–4400 and their Kyoto number is 075–371–5469. When outside these cities, you can also reach them free of charge via 0088–22–2800 (from the area around Tokyo and north-east of it; and 0088–22–4800 if you are anywhere west of Tokyo). They are open between 9 a.m. and 5 p.m. daily, *including* Sundays and public holidays.

Since Western books on Japan are much more expensive in Japan than in Western countries, it pays to stock up before setting out on your trip.

JAPAN'S HOMOGENEITY

Compared to most industrialized countries, the population of Japan (currently, approximately 124m.) is extremely homogeneous. Outside the large conurbations it is rare to find any foreigners. In the cities there are substantial numbers of Koreans and Chinese, but these do not generally differ in looks from the Japanese. In the entertainment districts, Thai, Burmese and Filipino girls are to be found (often illegally, trying to keep out of sight), and in odd jobs and other casual – often unpleasant – work you will see workers from a number of countries in Asia (again, often without state permission).

Due to the high cost of living in Japan, Western tourists have also diminished over the last few decades; but some may still be found in small numbers at the main sightseeing spots in Tokyo and Kyoto. In order to bump into Western businessmen, one would have to go to the main commercial areas of Tokyo (and, to a more limited extent, Osaka).

A WORD ABOUT JAPAN'S 'OUTSIDE WORLD'

The most important country by far for the majority of Japanese is the United States. In spite of a brutal war, many Japanese like the Americans and try to emulate some of their ways – at least superficially. Europeans are generally liked also, since many aspects of modernization were imported from Europe during the late nineteenth century.

Attitudes towards India and China tend to be mixed: – Buddhism and many other aspects of Japanese culture came from there, but during the first part of the twentieth century imperial ambitions made many Japanese feel superior – by no means a unique phenomenon among colonial powers.

'Internationalization' tends to be a buzz-word in today's Japan which has only superficial implications, such as importing a few (usually luxury) items from abroad to show how cosmopolitan one is.

International communication is hindered by the average Japanese person's inability to express ideas clearly in an international language, such as English, and the corresponding general inability by most Westerners to do the same in Japanese.

Top Tip

Many Japanese have never been abroad, and among those who have done so (other than businessmen), the most common way has been to join a tour group, for a very short period of time – for days rather than weeks. Since Japan is an island country, with Korea, China and Russia as her nearest neighbours, the feeling of 'us' versus 'them' is on the whole stronger than in other island countries like Britain which are so much closer to their continental neighbours.

ATTITUDES TOWARDS FOREIGNERS

The strong distinction made in Japan between 'inside' and 'outside' (see 'Understanding

Space', p.37) also pertains to 'gaikokujin' (lit. 'outside – country – person(s)'), often abbreviated to 'gaijin'. In the old days this may have tended to refer also to those Japanese not from one's native town or province, but an intensive and all-pervasive national unification drive in language, education, the media etc., plus an 'island mentality' and long seclusion in the past have given rise to a very strong 'We – the unique Japanese' feeling. This means that everyone else is on the 'outside', though at different levels of appreciation.

With the strong emphasis on hierarchy, Japanese tend to rank foreigners, with 'blue-eyed' 'white' Europeans and Americans at the top and Koreans generally at the bottom. Thus, visiting Europeans and Americans, especially if they speak (and even teach) the highly-regarded world language of English, can be assured of esteem. However, as many of these people have noticed perceptively, 'In Japan you are never made to forget that you are a visitor'.

2

Wining & Dining

'Noren' (short curtains) at the restaurant entrance

In Japan you will be offered Japanese tea (*o-cha*) at all hours as a matter of course. It is served hot without sugar or milk, in a teacup without a handle. This slightly bitter, green tea, refreshing once you are used to it, can be slurped (but don't overdo this).

If you venture out alone you may be refused entry into certain Japanese food/drink establishments. Most are like English clubs where newcomers (Japanese included) are required to be 'introduced' by regulars. Furthermore, the Japanese fear that you probably don't know enough about local customs to cope on your own. Don't be offended – this is rarely an anti-foreigner bias as such. Try instead to go with a Japanese friend or acquaintance and all should be well.

Top Tip

On being invited out to a Japanese meal and asked about your food preferences, it is usually best to say that anything will be alright, since it is the host's task to order. Such vagueness is not a sign that you are indiscriminate or indifferent: Japanese typically go along with their host's choice as well, preferring not to be different. If there are items in the selection that you find you don't like, then just leave them untouched and concentrate on the rest.

O-shibori

Before starting you may be handed a small folded towel (*o-shibori*), which is steamed hot in winter and is offered either hot or cold in summer. (You may well have been introduced to this splendid custom on your flight to Japan.) Take the towel from its sleeve and unfold it. Men can wipe their face with it, then their arms and hands. Women usually wipe their hands only. Later, during the meal, the o-shibori can be refolded and used to wipe your fingers.

Ideally, the meal starts when everyone bows slightly and says, *itadakimas'* ('I will receive') – rather like *bon appetit* in French.

If the meal is traditional Japanese food you can try and overcome your ignorance of conventional eating habits by taking the obvious course of imitating someone sitting close to you. If you are the guest of honour, you may have to start first, but after that it may be best simply to 'follow my leader'.

Dishes that look beautiful

Many Japanese dishes are served with the primary purpose of looking beautiful. But there are others, such as *tempura* (deep fried fish and vegetables) which are nutritious and appeal to Westerners probably because of their Western (Portuguese) origin. Even so, care will be taken to harmonize food shapes and colours with matching receptacles.

Further dishes, popular in Japan, which tend to appeal to Westerners are *sukiyaki* (vegetables and sliced beef, cooked at one's table) and *yakitori* (grilled chicken), since they are served hot. Various noodle dishes, such as *udon* and *soba* and Chinese noodles (*ramen*), are served either hot or cold, depending on the season. Japanese believe that slurping them with a loud noise enhances their flavour. Feel free to join in!

Rice is often the major ingredient of dishes, served in a deep bowl (*domburi*), where something else, such as broiled eel, or chicken and egg, is placed on the top. The former is called *unagi domburi* and the latter *oyako domburi* (lit.: parent and child).

Another inexpensive dish, popular with visitors, is *o-konomi-yaki* (lit. 'your favourite grill'), where batter is poured onto small pieces of beef or pork, prawns or various vegetables and prepared like an omelette by yourself on a hotplate in the middle of the table.

The list of Japanese foods obtained from the sea appears endless. If boiled or fried, the taste may be a familiar one, but when eaten raw it may be necessary to jump over one's own shadow. Perhaps the easiest introduction here is to start with *sushi* (raw bits of fish placed on top of vinegared rice) and *sashimi* (raw slivers of fish dipped into soy sauce and some hot horseradish).

Top Tip

To the uninitiated Western palate, a lot of Japanese food tastes rather bland. For Japanese it is not only the taste which is important, but also the food's consistency when felt with one's tongue inside the mouth (e.g. rice grains, slices of raw fish). Suspend your judgement at first (as with many things in Japan), and persevere. You might grow to enjoy judging food by criteria other than your own.

A proper Japanese meal always includes rice. Other dishes are added, depending on how elaborate the meal is. Instead of a succession of courses, most Japanese food is served all at once. The guest is then required to take small portions from each dish without neglecting any. Don't linger too long over one kind of food. Naturally, as a foreigner you can leave untouched any dish you don't like.

Before starting, remove the rice bowl lid and place it upside down on the left. Then put the soup bowl cover similarly on the right.

When at a public restaurant brand-new chopsticks (*hashi*) are provided; these are made of wood and split apart before use. Scrape one against the other to check for the absence of splinters. Pick up the chopsticks with your right hand and begin by eating the rice.

Chopsticks are really not that difficult to master, provided you put in some practice. Firstly, wedge the lower chopstick firmly in the crotch of your hand, holding it in place by the base of the thumb and the tip of the ring finger. It must not move! Then hold the upper chopstick quite independently, like a pen, between the tips of thumb, index finger and middle finger. Practice holding them one at a time. Then align both tips by pushing them against a flat surface. Try picking up objects by moving the upper tip onto the stationary lower one. Once adept at this, remember not to cross them on putting them down; neither stick them into the rice as a repository.

The art of holding chopsticks

You can lift the bowls containing rice (as well as soup) to your mouth with your left hand, for the purpose of eating the rice more efficiently.

If your rice bowl is empty, ask to have it filled from the large pot. As on all other occasions when giving or receiving something, it is polite to use both hands when lifting the bowl.

Rice left in your bowl indicates that you want more. To show that you have finished, pick out all the grains and eat them.

For dishes from which all guests can help themselves, use the special chopsticks or spoons provided. If absent, reverse your own chopsticks and transfer the food with the clean ends.

Replace the covers of the bowls, and place the chopsticks side-by-side onto the rice bowls or on the special ceramic chopstick rest provided.

Finally, say *gochisō-sama-desh'ta* ('It was a feast', or 'Many thanks for the meal') on leaving, and bow slightly.

Items associated with Saké

Whenever alcohol is served, raise your glass or cup to have it filled, and take a sip before putting it down. Offer to serve others of your party if they have served you: ideally, one never pours one's own drinks.

As a sign of esteem or friendship you may be offered another guest's *saké* cup. Accept it with thanks, and raise it to be filled. Later (not immediately) you can offer your cup after having cleaned it, and pour *saké* in return.

Top Tip

The Japanese toast for 'your health' is *kampai* (lit. 'a dry cup'). Incidentally, beer (and occasionally wine) is increasingly drunk instead of *saké* at a Japanese meal. Your empty cup or glass signals to your host that you would like it filled; leave the glass or cup full, therefore, if you don't want any more to drink.

If invited to a bar or night club, enjoy the relaxed atmosphere. Refrain from talking shop and be prepared to sing a few songs when the microphone is passed your way. (See 'Karaoke Business' p.62.) Some party tricks come in handy here, or the showing of photographs from back home. Don't attempt to pay or offer to 'go Dutch'. However, reciprocate later with some gift, or a counter-invitation to a Western restaurant. (But, be warned, Western-style restaurants in Japan can be prohibitively expensive.)

If there are hostesses, the one whose English is best will probably be assigned to you, but don't expect this flirtatious atmosphere to lead to anything more. Further insights into the intricacies, etiquette and customs of Japanese night-life are best obtained from 'old hands' and numerous books on this topic!

Alcohol tends to affect Japanese more quickly and drunkenness does not carry the same stigma as in the West. However, it may be reassuring to know that drunks in the evening entertainment districts tend, on the whole, to be good-natured and may even insist on further pub-crawling (sometimes with all expenses paid) with the foreigner whom they met a few minutes ago. In that case you might enjoy the experience, and reciprocate by trying to hail a taxi for them at the end of the evening and sending a thank-you letter from your home town.

On the other hand, some drunks can occasion-ally turn nasty when they see a foreigner and start being abusive. In such a case it is prudent to stay well clear. Furthermore, since some Japanese have weak stomachs, you should take care not to stand too close to drunks – for obvious reasons.

3

The Japanese Home

'genkan'

As a businessman it will be a rare event to enter your host's home.* Some major reasons for this are the following:

• The average Japanese home is much smaller than those in the West and is rarely open to non-kin.

• Entertaining, even of kin, usually takes place outside the home, in one of the many restaurants, coffee shops, or bars.

• The housewife is usually concerned that her conversational English is poor or non-existent.

---

* It is entirely possible, if you so wish, to arrange a Japanese 'homestay' through one of the organizations which specializes in this service. The TIC (see p.20) can advise you here.

- There is the further worry that the foreigner is probably unfamiliar with Japanese customs, e.g. sitting on *tatami* (traditional rectangular, finely-woven straw) mats, using the squat-type toilet, etc.
- The house may be far from the town, so that visitors could have problems returning to their hotel in the evening.

However, if you *do* get invited, try to remember the following:

Top Tip

On entering the house, remove your shoes in the hallway (*genkan*) before stepping up to the floor of the house proper. Slippers will be provided, although they are often quite small. Before entering any room laid out with *tatami* mats, leave the slippers behind and proceed in stockinged feet. Treat the *tatami* floor as though it were one large mattress – in such case it makes sense to remove one's footwear!

On or before entering the toilet, look out for the special slippers (often marked 'W.C.') and change into these. Don't forget to change back to regular slippers on leaving the toilet! Since you must always backtrack to recover slippers and shoes, Japanese houses make you feel tied to an invisible rubber band anchored at the *genkan*.

Squatting on one's legs (Japan's traditional 'sitting' posture) can be painful, even for today's young Japanese who are used to chairs. You can therefore sit cross-legged (if male), but females (except in jeans) should fold their legs under their bodies, then move the weight off to one side. In some traditional-style rooms there is a recess in the floor (which contains a heater in winter – *kotatsu*) that is deep enough for your legs. There you can sit almost as if on a chair, especially if a legless back-rest is provided.

The fact is that one also has to squat over the Japanese-style toilet – uncomfortable, but hygienic. The water container above it (which one faces on squatting) allows you to wash your hands under the faucet which curves over the bowl-shaped lid. The lever hanging down can be pushed left or right, so that either all the water is released or just a small amount – a convenient way to save water.

Sitting cross-legged

Sometimes the toilet door cannot be locked. Japanese determine whether a toilet is engaged by knocking gently on the outside door, and then wait for a counter-knock to emanate. Unknowing Westerners, once inside, sometimes use their body weight in desperation to stop others from entering. The latter, in turn, might think that the door is stuck, and push all the more... This 'counter-knocking' custom naturally assumes that the distance between toilet and door is a short one!

The *tokonoma*

UNDERSTANDING SPACE

If one compares a Japanese person's house (or even country) to one's own body, the stronger distinction in Japan between what is 'inside' and what is 'outside' may start to make sense to a Western onlooker. 'Outside' is strange and does not really concern one very much, while 'inside' is 'intimate', 'cozy', calling for a different kind of behaviour.

Inside the house one is greeted by standard phrases, and replies in a specified way that one is entering, one changes outdoor shoes for indoor slippers (see p.32), etc. Inside partitionings are thin, often movable, and do not screen out sounds from adjacent rooms. This is how Japanese children are brought up, with the ability to tolerate cooperative living in a small space, able to 'look away' and 'listen away' if necessary.

THE JAPANESE BATH

To appreciate the qualities of a Japanese-style bath fully you need to take your time and combine cleanliness with relaxation. The bath (o-furo) is therefore ideally in a different room from the toilet.

Undress in the antechamber and place your clothes in one of the baskets provided. Pick up a small towel and enter the bathroom. If others are present, use the towel to hide your nakedness a little. Get a washing bowl and soap, and squat down on a small stool. Scoop some hot water from the tub. Soap your body and rub it, using the towel. Ladle hot water over yourself from the tub, taking care not to get any soap into it.

o-furo

Of course you need not enter the tub at all, but if you do want to try it, cool part of your anatomy by putting the cold, dripping towel on top of your head. Submerge up to your neck as quickly as possible and then sit quite still – after a few agonizing seconds the pain will subside somewhat. Totally immobile, you might even start enjoying this foetal state! Once adapted, stay inside as long as you like, or alternate this with further washing outside.

After leaving the tub, wring the towel and dry yourself with it – this works surprisingly well. If provided, put on the cotton gown (*yukata*) over your underwear. Take care to wrap the left side over the right, which is customary for both sexes. The reverse is used only once –i.e., when you are laid out for the wake, before cremation! Worn with a sash (*obi*), the yukata (provided in all hotels) now serves as a dressing-gown and/or night-gown.

yukata

4

Gift-giving

Japanese gift-giving is a highly ritualized custom, used mainly as a 'social lubricant' to smooth social interaction. Fortunately, foreigners need not participate fully, but their gifts will be appreciated, leading to return gifts. Three major rules are thus worth remembering:

● GIFTS SHOULD ALWAYS BE WRAPPED. For your unwrapped gift, get a Japanese friend's help with gift paper and special string. Or buy some gifts in a Japanese shop and ask for your 'naked' gifts to be wrapped as well. You can get fancy paper and ribbons at stationery-shops (*bunbōgu-ya*).

● A GIFT, ONCE OFFERED, CANNOT BE REFUSED, except if it 'smells' like a bribe, in which case it should be returned as soon as possible. Japanese usually belittle their (wrapped) gifts when presenting them. The 'unworthy' receiver should in turn express reluctance and initially hesitate to accept. However, this ritualized exchange has only one outcome which is never in doubt. As a foreigner you need not belittle your gift, but don't praise it, either.

● JAPANESE TRADITIONALLY DON'T OPEN THE GIFT IN THE PRESENCE OF THE GIVER. This allows face to be saved if the gift is much more (or less) expensive than announced. However, if urged to open your gift, you can do so.

Take care not to give too valuable a gift, since equally expensive return presents are usually required of the receiver. This can continue indefinitely, making it very burdensome (and expensive). A gift's major function is not, 'I have plenty, so let's share ...', or, 'This is for you as a unique individual'. Rather, gifts serve as a balancing of obligations and a continued reminder of the importance of the relationship. Japanese are more finicky here than we are. Get an insider's view if in doubt what to give initially, and what to return.

On receiving a gift, some Japanese might give you a *token return gift* of low value. It is a kind of 'receipt' for your gift – the real return gift will come later. Material gifts can also be given for non-material favours. Get advice whether they are regarded as 'balancing'.

Top Tip

Before departure, try to buy a number of gifts in your home town, ranging from expensive to inexpensive. Small mementos (even picture post-cards of your town) are appreciated as tokens of kindness shown. If you come from an historic town or one famous for particular products, then purchase a variety of 'souvenirs' to take with you. These will be extremely useful gifts and will be much appreciated. At the top of the list high-quality whisky is a good gift, though bulky and heavy. Buy *boxed* bottles and take the maximum allowed (currently three per person).

Tax-free shops in airports from which there is a direct air connection with Japan usually stock these boxed bottles. *Chivas Regal* as well as rare malt whisky is preferred. *Napoleon Brandy* is also a good (but expensive) buy. However, whisky bottles bought on the plane to Japan are often not boxed, and the bottles are often made of cheap-looking plastic. If this is all you can get, due to a last-minute rush, at least ask a Japanese acquaintance to wrap them nicely in gift paper after your arrival.

Luxury foods (from the UK – quality marmalade or tea for example) also make good gifts, especially if you are likely to be introduced to the wives of Japanese businessmen. If you run out of such gifts you can usually re-stock at Japanese department stores, though at substantially higher prices.

Crabtree & Evelyn as well as Fortnum & Mason brand goods are relatively hard to get in Japan, and thus regarded more highly than gifts by many other makers. Other gifts can include Wedgwood porcelain (though heavy and breakable), ties, commemorative coins, coffee-table books of your town or area, as well as toy models (e.g. of London buses) for your host's children. Cufflinks may be less appropriate as gifts, since not many Japanese men wear them.

Most Japanese are keen photographers and will want to take photographs of their friends in a group. Colour prints are subsequently given as small gifts to those in the picture as a matter of courtesy. When you photograph acquaintances and friends in turn, it is a good idea to present them with copies.

Top Tip

Don't admire some art object excessively in your hosts' house – they might feel they should present it to you!

5

Out & About

THE PUBLIC TRANSPORT SYSTEM

While queues tend to be orderly, helped greatly by the fact that the positions of individual train doors are clearly marked on station platforms, wholesale shoving can occur during rush hours just before the doors are closed. It is then not unusual to see aspiring passengers barging into the bulging multitude at the open door as if it were a rugby scrum. Inside, it is uncommon for younger persons to stand up for older ones, let alone pregnant women.

When the bus or carriage is full it is best to hang onto one's strap and doze while standing. There is often no space for holding a book or paper in front of one's eyes. Frequent announcements over the public address system alert passengers to the name of the next station. Sometimes, there is also the useful information concerning the side of the train on which the next station's platform will be. Announcements tend to be in Japanese only, except on the 'bullet train' Shinkansen (lit. 'New Trunk Line').

The Shinkansen routes

There is limited time for getting out, so even before the train has stopped it is wise to wriggle past other passengers. On advancing it is polite to extend a partly outstretched arm in front of the body, with the palm held vertically, waving the arm up and down and bowing slightly at the same time, saying 'sumimasen' ('excuse me') or 'shitsurei shimas' ('I am being rude').

There is lots of eating and drinking on long-distance transport. On trains there are frequent trolley services, including offers of miniature whisky bottles with glasses, e.g. on the Shinkansen. Occasionally, cleaners make their rounds with large plastic bags into which leftovers can be deposited.

Eating and drinking is frowned on in commuter trains and buses. Neither is smoking permitted. Increasingly, smoking is also being restricted on train platforms, especially during rush hours. There are 'kitsuen-kōna' on some platforms, where smoking is permitted.

'SHOULDER SLEEPERS'

In trains, especially late at night, many passengers fall asleep while sitting upright. They then tend to slew over to one side. Should someone be sitting next to them, the sleepers' heads will come to rest on their neighbours' shoulders. This seems to be tolerated by many Japanese, perhaps because it is seen as a permissible regression to early childhood. If somebody falls asleep on your shoulder, you might enjoy the experience of anonymity coupled with closeness.

The author once even experienced two heads resting on each one of his shoulders! He felt rather embarrassed having to get off at his destination, thereby causing the two sleepers to suffer from a sudden withdrawal shock.

VISITORS AND THE POLICE

Well-behaved visitors need not fear unpleasant encounters with the Japanese police, provided they do not bring any prohibited drugs (e.g. marijuana) into the country, and as long as they carry their passport as identification on them *at all times*.

Top Tip

There are many police boxes (*kōban*) in Japanese cities, manned around the clock, whose policemen know the surrounding area well and who are prepared to assist with the finding of elusive neighbourhood addresses (which sometimes can be very elusive indeed!).

YOUTH AND LEISURE

Unlike Western culture, with its Christianity-derived attitude of 'either – or', Japanese morality tends to favour the 'both – and' approach. That is to say, provided one works hard during a specified time, one can enjoy oneself during the after-hours.

Young people are generally encouraged to strive for the highest academic achievement they are capable of. This is being assessed throughout their teens by a successive mountain of entrance tests allowing or barring entrance to the next higher institution. Thus, little time remains for individual pursuits, since schools also require pupils to participate in team efforts until late in the day, as well as on many holidays. Furthermore, much time is taken up during afternoons and evenings by cram schools (jūkū), voluntarily attended, which allow better preparation for the next entrance test.

However, once having successfully entered a university, students can finally take it much more easy in general than the average Western undergraduate, since, within the Japanese system, their future employment chances tend to be more contingent on their university's public standing than individual scores at graduation.

Having graduated in their early twenties, most Japanese males join a company and from then onwards enjoy restricted time of their own. Females, on the other hand, often take on less demanding work (either by choice, or due to sex discrimination at the work place). Since many of them still live with their parents, a lot of their savings can be used for leisure travel during their holidays, and this includes travel overseas. Therefore, the Japanese tourists you are likely to meet around the world tend to be unmarried females in their twenties, or retired persons travelling in organized groups.

GAMBLING AND THE *YAKUZA*

Yakuza are tightly-organized gangsters, living from extortion rackets, such as prostitution. Recent changes in Japanese law have curbed their activities somewhat, but *yakuza* can still be most obnoxious. They are often dressed in snazzy Western clothes and drive very large American cars. If you see them from nearby, you might try to establish their identity for sure by looking to see if they have lost the top of their pinkie.

The good news is that they rarely set out to bother foreign businessmen, or foreigners in general for that matter, so you are unlikely to come across them. If you do – try to stay clear! *Yakuza* are often involved with gambling joints, such as pachinko parlours (see below).

Pachinko facility

PACHINKO?

As mentioned under taboo subjects (pages 57-58), the Western visitor is often granted a 'fool's licence' concerning conversation topics which can be discussed. This may also apply to requests. If the desire to play *pachinko* with Japanese business colleagues is suggested, for example, they may either agree and go there with you, or mention some excuse, but they will rarely reply that this is a foolish idea. Many of these 'amusements' (including pub-crawling, consorting with bar hostesses, etc.) are regarded as perfectly legitimate fun as long as they are carried out at the right time (i.e. mostly after hours) and with proper decorum. On meeting again for business, in a sober state, it is good manners to say 'thanks for the other day/last night', but not by going into details.

6

Conversation & Communication

'. . . lengthy monologues are common'

Japanese tend not to come to the point straight away, which you might find very tedious at first. After formal introductions, green tea will normally be served. This is a good time for small talk when contentious topics should be avoided. The main topic may be broached much later, or perhaps not at all during the first meeting. Have patience!

Don't be dogmatic in your statements – it is rude to be too direct. Get used to vague and indirect replies, and sense if an atmosphere of mutual trust is developing. If not, try to postpone the discussion of serious matters instead of forcing the issue.

During formal business meetings lengthy monologues – often by the senior person present –
are common. If you speak, try to make more
pauses than usual so that your Japanese partners
can contribute if they want to. Even interpreters,
when present, may have trouble understanding
you fully without showing it, so check frequently if
your point has come across, but without making
them look foolish.

Top Tip

Don't use first names for addressing your Japanese
partners; rather use 'Mr/Mrs/Miss/Dr X' instead.
Alternatively, use their family name, plus -*san* for
everyone except academics, who can be addressed
as *sensei* ('teacher'). If you were already on first-
name terms with somebody before arrival in Japan,
you should discuss whether to continue this, but it is
safer to use family name and -*san* in the presence of
others.

Don't be alarmed if you are addressed by your
first name and -*san*. Some Japanese believe
they can be less formal with foreigners (and you
should reciprocate). Alternatively, it may be
assumed to be your family name, since in Japan
family name precedes given name. If you have an
unusual given name, avoid confusion by printing it
in initials only before your family name on your
business cards, or printing your family name larger
than your given name.

Try to tone down expressions of displeasure,
keep a calm face and don't raise your voice.

Even then you will probably still appear to be more volatile than most Japanese.

On being introduced to non-English speakers it will sound better if you say something complimentary in your own language than if you utter nothing at all. It is the friendly *intonation* which counts, together with your smile and slight bow.

UNDERSTANDING SILENCE

Those Westerners who come to Japan looking for a 'culture of silence' may be sorely disappointed. In fact, there is a lot of preventable 'noise pollution': traffic, sirens, barking dogs, thin walls, etc. Even Zen gardens may have loudspeakers hidden in the bushes to provide 'relevant comments'. However, in personal interaction there may be a lot of silence at times when Westerners would feel the urge to explain.

On the whole, more things in daily life are taken for granted by the Japanese, so in predictable circumstances fewer explanations are necessary. Towards foreigners, being tongue-tied is not necessarily regarded as a disadvantage, especially since the Japanese language has many stock phrases which can be used with good effect, instead of trying to 'make conversation' by trying to say something original.

Photos of your family and home town in a pocket-size album make a good conversation piece, especially if you have language problems. A small dictionary and blank paper are handy to have interesting objects explained to you. Furthermore, you can ask to be taught paper folding (*origami*). In Japan, many activities we consider child-like (or even 'childish') are quite respectable, especially while alcohol is being consumed. On the other hand, a grown-up licking a large ice-cream cone in public looks 'childish' to most Japanese.

tsuru (crane) – origami version

Top Tip

If you do step on Japanese toes (and this is sometimes unavoidable), at least try to convey the sincere impression that you are sorry. If stuck for Japanese words, using English is better than saying nothing at all, together with the appropriate gestures. Remember to apologize often, even for seemingly trivial mistakes. *Sumimasen* expresses general regret.

When making verbal decisions, especially over the phone, there is always the chance of being misunderstood. You may have trouble with the Japanized version of English words. One reason is the rule in Japanese that a consonant is followed by a vowel (rather like

Italian). This can turn 'taxi' into *takushii*, etc. Conversely, rapidly-spoken 'British'-English can be misunderstood because American pronunciation is more widely used in Japan.

A lways speak clearly and relatively slowly, but not insultingly so. Although most Japanese can read and correspond in English, they have little occasion to speak it. Therefore, avoid dialect, slang words, or puns. Don't raise your voice when misunderstood – either repeat your words slowly, or write them down if they are of importance.

B ecause of the value given to politeness, Japanese don't like you and others to realize that they frequently don't understand what you say even if they look as if they do. However, keep in mind that their understanding of your culture and language is likely to be much greater than yours is of theirs.

D on't be put off if long pauses occur in a conversation. To most Japanese, using Eng-lish for any length of time is very tiring. The overall response time to a question may also be longer. Silences in conversation produce less anxiety than in the West. Avoid repeating your question with a raised voice, and try to listen more than usual. (See 'Understanding Silence', p.54.)

D on't defend your point of view vehemently, thereby putting your partner in the wrong. Japanese will tend to agree with others just for the sake of preserving harmony – what they really think is another matter. In Japan this is not hypocrisy, but good manners.

There is a large amount of implicit trust in Japan, especially if you have had an introduction to some group. Questions are usually phrased in such a way that you can give an affirmative answer. Except for vital business decisions, you can often agree to something without having understood the question fully, and then hope for the best. Getting back to a child-like state of trust could be one of the many pleasant experiences of visiting Japan.

TABOO TOPICS?

Being a short-term visitor, you are generally allowed a fool's licence concerning awkward questions. Almost anything can be discussed, except making disparaging remarks about the Japanese Emperor. However, if you mention immigration, sex, political corruption etc. do not automatically expect a straight or truthful reply. Japanese politeness towards high-status persons, coupled with the desire not to make anyone lose face, will tend to result in bland and non-committal answers.

Remember, too, that most Japanese have simply not given much thought to many of those problems which are regularly discussed in the West in public, so they simply may not know the correct answer. In spite of having this fool's licence, Western visitors are still advised to avoid potentially awkward questions and to behave in a civilized fashion where one tries not to embarrass one's hosts.

Emperor Akihito & Empress Michiko

7

Business Matters

Introductions to a new business contact important to you, should ideally be made by a respected and trustworthy go-between who knows both parties.

Dress well, but conservatively, avoiding flashy colours. The Japanese for 'suit' is *'sebiro'*, which comes from the name 'Savile Row', London. Allied with this is good deportment; too relaxed a bearing can be interpreted as a sign of a 'crooked spirit'.

Since the Japanese value group solidarity, be prepared to be met on arrival and seen off at departure. This holds for important Japanese visitors as well. However, instead of a rendezvous at far-off Narita Airport (65 kms. from central Tokyo) you might suggest the Tokyo City Air Terminal (TCAT), about 2.5 kilometres from Tokyo Station, which has direct bus connections and check-in facilities.

Separated from their reference group, Japanese tend to telephone or write back to base frequently, even if there is little news. This is seen as necessary to continue smooth relations. There is no harm in copying this custom with your Japanese group, especially after you return home. Cards at Christmas and New Year and copies of group photos are good reminders that you still care.

When introduced, Japanese businessmen will first exchange business cards (*meishi*). It pays to have your own right at the start of your visit, ideally with a translation in Japanese on the reverse. Check with your airline about this service well before departure. (There could be a 3–4 week delay in obtaining them.) Cards can often be picked up on arrival in Japan. If you are unable to arrange for cards to be printed, buy blank cards and use your rubber stamp or stick-on address labels as a temporary substitute.

Exchanging *meishi*

Top Tip

When ushered into a room, sit at the place allocated by your host, since the seat of honour and other positions in decreasing order of importance are usually predetermined, especially in the traditional Japanese house.

After shaking hands or bowing, hand over your business card with a slight bow, receiving one in return from your new acquaintance who may hiss through his teeth while studying your card. This shows that you are an important person. Take your time to study the card received, and ask for a translation of it, if it is in Japanese only. Once seated, you can keep it in view on the table or on the arm-rest of your chair. Finally, take the trouble to pocket it with some indication that it is of value to you. Special albums are available at stationers to keep such cards sorted for future reference.

'. . . be prepared to sing a few songs'

KARAOKE BUSINESS

A recent cultural export from Japan is *karaoké* (from *kara* = 'empty' and *oké* = short for 'orchestra'), where groups of usually inebriated party members take turns to sing popular songs in time to canned music. In Japan, it is often a recreation enjoyed by businessmen with colleagues and/or clients, in their favourite bars. Here it is not the individual singing ability which counts, but the willingness to pick up a microphone and to pretend to be a great singer.

The generous applause at the end (either by your doting friends, or even built into the tape at the end of your song) should not lead you to believe that you have a great voice: in Japan everyone tends to get a prize. It is rather the willingness to make a fool of yourself in front of the group which is likely to be appreciated.

Once everybody has gone through this ritual, the ice is broken and the party can continue at a more intimate level. It pays to know one or two standard songs such as 'My Way' beforehand, but frequently words will be supplied, sometimes even with laser disc on a tv screen where appropriate background pictures are shown to match the music.

Most Japanese businessmen will have endured/ enjoyed several years on English instruction at schools and university. However, this will largely have comprised the reading and translating of English only, rather like Latin or Greek was drummed into the heads of pre-war Western schoolchildren, leaving most of them unable to carry on with an impromptu conversation.

However, many of the people you are likely to meet in the context of Japanese business have been specially chosen to interact with foreigners. Here the use and knowledge of English has increased over the last few years.

Remember to speak slowly and clearly; remember also that many misunderstandings are possible, to be remedied only by a lengthy study of Japanese thought and behaviour patterns, which cannot be dealt with here.

Japanese generally prefer discussing business in the hotel's reception area and not in your bedroom. If unacceptable, suggest moving to a coffee shop or bar. Most Japanese seem to accept that they can be overheard by strangers in such places.

Taxi drivers sometimes have trouble finding an address. When lost, they often enquire at a police box (*kōban*), but this is time-consuming. You can help by requesting written instructions in Japanese or a sketch from your host beforehand. Otherwise ask at your hotel's front desk (*furonto*) for written instructions. Communication by fax is therefore popular and widespread in Japan.

Top Tip

The Japanese '*furonto*' means the reception desk (abbreviation of 'front desk') and not the front (or exit) of a hotel – a possible cause for serious misunderstanding when trying to meet in Japan.

WOMEN AND BUSINESS

More than in Western industrialized countries, Japanese women tend to be discriminated against in their workplace, despite legal guarantees to the contrary. Western businesswomen can therefore expect to meet few, if any of their counterparts in Japan and may themselves be viewed as an oddity in overwhelmingly male-dominated surroundings of business and after-hours entertainment.

Similar to her Western male colleagues, a Western businesswoman during her initial stay is likely to be treated as a high-status *gaijin no o-kyakyu-sama* (honourable foreign guest) first and foremost; only secondly as a female who can be openly or subtly discriminated against; and thirdly as an unwelcome obstacle, to be avoided.

However, even in the role of guest she might not be invited to after-hours drinking sessions as easily as her male colleagues, especially not to more intimate parties involving female entertainers which high-status visitors and important clients might get asked to after the evening's rather formal initial party.

On the other hand, Japan has a long history of little or no molestation of women who venture out alone in public, compared to many other oriental countries. However, during parties, Japanese males, pleading drunkenness, may sometimes start fondling or pinching Western

A welcome from the lift-attendant

women. If the latter create a fuss promptly, this should ideally lead to apologies and no further contact. Similar molestation does occur on crowded trains. Here, protestations might be useless, as Japanese bystanders tend to pretend that nothing untoward is happening.

Since Japanese wives are mostly excluded when their husbands entertain on business, Western wives are rarely invited either. However, due to gradual 'internationalization' of some areas of Japanese business life, Western and other 'foreign' wives are increasingly being invited to more formal functions. If they go, they should not expect to be engaged in scintillating conversation by their (usually) tongue-tied male Japanese hosts. Neither are they very likely to meet the wives of such persons.

8

Useful Phrases & Vocabulary

KON-NICHIWA!

Written Japanese is difficult; but elementary spoken Japanese can be acquired easily as will be seen in the sister volume to this book *Very Simple Japanese*. However, you will create a good impression if you make the effort to learn just a few phrases and words. The following are amongst those frequently required by the visitor:-

Mr/Mrs/Miss	. . . **san** *after* the surname (but don't ever add -san to your own name).
Good morning	**ohayō gozaimas'**
Good day	**kon-nichi wa**

Good evening	**konban wa**
Good bye	**Sayōnara**
Good night (on retiring)	**O-yasumi nasai**
Hot, isn't it!	**atsui des' nē!**
Cold, isn't it!	**samui des' nē!**
Yes, I am listening	**hai, hai**
Yes, I agree	**hai, sō des'**
No (rarely used)	**ii-e**
No, I disagree	**chigaimas'**
Please (help yourself)	**dōzo**
Please give me . . .	**. . . o kudasai**
On starting a meal	**itadakimas'**
Cheers!	**kampai!**
Thank you (for kindness)	**dōmo arigatō gozaimash'ta**
Thank you (after a meal)	**gochisō-sama desh'ta**
Thanks (for recent kindness shown)	**kono aida wa dōmo arigatō gozaimash'ta**
No thank you (I have had enough)	**mō kekko des'**
Excuse me (or: I am sorry)	**sumimasen**
It's all right	**daijōbu des'**
My name is . . .	**. . . des'** (*after* your surname)
Pleased to meet you	**dōzo yoroshiku**
You're welcome	**dō itashimash'te**
No, thank YOU	**ii-e kochira koso**
Pleased to meet you (*formal style*)	**hajimemash'te, o-me ni kakarimas'**
Where is . . . ?	**. . . wa doko des'ka?**
Please give me . . .	**. . . o kudasai**
How much does it cost?	**. . . wa ikura des'ka?**
I don't understand	**wakarimasen**

Who speaks English?	**dare ka eigo o hanasemas'ka?**
I don't understand Japanese	**Nihongo ga wakarimasen**
Please call a taxi	**takushii o yonde kudasai**
I want to go . . .	**. . . ni ikitai des' ga**
This is the address	**kore ga jūsho des'**
To the right	**migi**
To the left	**hidari**
Straight ahead	**massugu**
Stop	**tomatte**
Here	**koko**
There	**asoko**
Faster	**motto hayaku**
More slowly	**motto yukkuri**

Pronunciation:

Vowels similar to Italian or German:

a as in *far*
e as in *men*
i as in *meet*
o as in *gone*
u as in *put*

Consonant as in English except:
g as in 'give' at the start of a word, otherwise **ng** as in 'sing'
s always hard, as in 'see'

Vowels written here with a macron (¯) should be pronounced at two times the normal length. Words featuring an apostrophe (e.g. **des'**): the apostrophe replaces the vowel '**u**' or '**i**', which is not pronounced.

Japanese Words Used In This Book
(page references in italics)

bunbōgu-ya *40*	stationery shop
daruma *18*	used as a 'good luck' token with second eye filled in if project is successful
domburi *27*	deep bowl
furonto *64*	front desk of hotel
gaijin *22, 65*	foreigner (especially Westerner)
genkan *34*	vestibule or entrance hallway of a Japanese house
gochisō-sama-desh'ta *30*	'It was a feast' (said after finishing a meal)
hai, hai *18*	indicates that the person you are talking to is still listening
hanko *75*	chop seal with a Japanese person's name, etc.
hashi *28*	chopsticks
ii-e *60*	no! (rarely used)
itadakimas' *26*	like the French *bon appetit*, said before starting a meal
kamo shiremasen *60*	'well, maybe'
kampai *31*	a toast, similar to 'cheers!'
karaoké *62*	sing-along music machine
kitsuen kōna *47*	corner in stations where smoking is permitted

kōban *48, 64*	police box, manned round the clock
meishi *61*	business card
noren *24*	short curtains displayed at entrance to shops, restaurants
obi *39*	a long sash worn with Japanese kimono or yukata
o-cha *24*	Japanese green tea
o-furo *38*	Japanese bath
o-konomi-yaki *27*	various ingredients in batter, fried by customers on their own hot plate
o-kyaku-sama *65*	way to address an honoured guest
origami *55*	the art of folding paper into shapes
o-shibori *26*	hot or cold small towel
oyako-domburi *27*	chicken and egg on top of rice, served in a deep bowl
pachinko *50*	pinball game
ramen *27*	Chinese noodles
saké *31*	alcoholic beverage made from fermented rice
-san *53*	address form for Japanese, except children, irrespective of gender; follows the family name
sashimi *27*	sliced raw fish

sebiro *59*	Western style men's suit (word derived from London's 'Savile Row')
sensei *53*	address of respect to a teacher or senior person
Shinkansen *46*	'bullet train', lit.: New Trunk Line
shitsurei shimas' *47*	'I am being rude'
soba *27*	buckwheat noodles
sukiyaki *27*	vegetables and sliced beef, cooked on the dining table
sumimasen *47, 55*	'excuse me', word of apology
sushi *27*	raw bits of fish etc. on top of a ball of vinegared rice
takushii *55*	taxi
tatami *34*	thick rectangular straw mats covered with woven rush
tempura *26*	deep-fried fish and vegetables
tokonoma *36*	alcove in a home usually containing hanging scroll and flower arrangement
udon *27*	noodles made from wheat flour
unagi domburi *27*	broiled eel on top of rice, served in a deep bowl
yakitori *27*	grilled bits of chicken etc.
yakuza *49*	gangster
yukata *38*	light buttonless cotton gown, worn with a sash

Facts About Japan

Japan is formed by an archipelago of over 3,000 islands, the four largest being Honshu (231,000 sq. km.), Hokkaido (83,500 sq. km), Kyushu (42,000 sq. km.) and Shikoku (19,000 sq. km.). (see map p. 8)

The Japanese islands are 70% covered in forest, which is strictly protected.

Only 15% of the Japanese land surface is level enough to be used for human habitation.

The capital, Tokyo, has a population of almost 12 million. Other major cities include: Yokohama (3.2 million), Osaka (2.4 million), Nagoya (2.0 million) and Sapporo (1.7 million).

The climate of Japan is generally mild, but since the country stretches some 3,000km there can be a wide variance. The north of the country shares the same latitude as Quebec, Canada, and the south as Key West, Florida.

THE SEASONS OF JAPAN

The table below gives the average seasonal temperatures (centigrade) and number of rainy days for Sapporo, on the northernmost island of Hokkaido, Tokyo, and Kagoshima, on the southernmost island of Kyushu (see map p. 8)

	JANUARY			APRIL			JULY			OCTOBER		
	High	Low	Rain	High	Low	Rain	High	Low	Rain	High	Low	Rain
Sapporo	-1.1	-8.4	17	11.1	2.2	8	24.8	16.6	8	15.7	6.0	12
Tokyo	9.5	1.2	4	18.3	10.3	10	28.8	22.3	10	21.2	14.2	9
Kagoshima	12.2	2.6	10	21.3	11.8	12	31.4	24.2	12	25.1	15.3	7

The four seasons in most of Japan including Tokyo and Kyoto are **Spring** – March, April, May; **Summer** – June, July, August; **Autumn** – September, October, November; **Winter** – December, January, February. The rainy season is from mid-June to mid-July. Though the humidity rises, there is no squall-type rain. The typhoon season is mostly confined to September. Tropical low atmospheric pressure areas developing into typhoons in the southern Pacific occasionally hit the Japanese islands in their northern advance, sometimes causing delays to transportation systems.

Japan uses the Metric system of weights and measures.

While Japan has the lowest voltage in the world (100V), the country operates two different electric cycles: 50 cycles in eastern Japan (including Tokyo) and 60 cycles in western Japan, including Nagoya, Kyoto and Osaka.

The tap water is safe to drink throughout Japan.

Japan has a highly developed rail system, and is justly proud of its high-speed inter-city train, the *Shinkansen* (popularly known as the 'bullet' train). Tokyo has an extensive subway system, and subways also operate in eight other cities, including Osaka and Nagoya.

While Japanese drive on the left (as in the UK) most imported luxury cars are specifically ordered with left-hand drive, so that the 'exotic' vehicles are made to look even more so.

National Holidays

New Year's Day	1 January
Coming-of-Age Day	15 January
Commemoration of the Founding of the Nation	11 February
Vernal Equinox Day	*around* 21 March
Greenery Day	29 April
Constitution Day	3 May
Children's Day	5 May
(when 3 May and 5 May fall on weekdays 4 May is also regarded as a holiday)	
Marine Day	20 July
Respect-for-the-Aged Day	15 September
Autumnal Equinox	*around* 23 September
Health-Sports Day	10 October
Culture Day	3 November
Labour-Thanksgiving Day	23 November
Emperor's Birthday	3 December

Japanese currency consists of 10,000 yen, 5,000 yen and 1,000 yen notes and 500 yen, 100 yen, 50 yen, 10 yen, 5 yen and 1 yen coins.

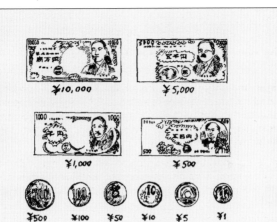

Japanese currency

HOW TO EXCHANGE MONEY

All banks displaying an Authorized Foreign Exchange sign can change your money at that day's exchange rate. Banks operate their exchange counters from 9 a.m. to 3 p.m. Monday to Friday. Ensure you have your passport with you when converting traveller's cheques. Processing may take some time for large sums and certain currencies; check these details in advance. Many major hotels and large department stores also offer exchange services, but note that these may charge a handling fee and reqire passport identification for all transactions.

Credit Cards are widely accepted in urban areas, but are not as popular as in Europe or the USA, and should not be relied upon for travel in more remote areas. Yen travellers' cheques may be purchased at European or US banks. There is virtually no use of personal cheques.

Japanese are by law only allowed to have one first (or given) name.

Within their own society, Japanese do not use signatures. Instead, they make use of chop seals (or name seals) which print their family name. Such *hanko* need to be carried around when conducting any business requiring a signature (e.g. on visiting a bank). They are often handed to the clerk, who does the appropriate stamping.

Banks are open from 9a.m.-3p.m. Monday to Friday, and are closed on national holidays. Post offices are generally open from 9a.m.-5p.m. Monday to Friday, and are closed on national holidays, although some main post offices open every day.

Most large shops and department stores are open from 10a.m.-7 or 8p.m. everyday (including Sundays and Holidays) although some department stores may close one day a week.

THE TELEPHONE SERVICE

Public telephones are generously distributed throughout Japan and of three types: yellow, green and red. All three accept 10 yen coins, yellow and green also accept 100 yen coins and green ones also take phone cards. These may be purchased at NTT Customer Service Centres, or at shops and vending machines situated near public telephones.

Emergency phone numbers: Police 100, Fire & Ambulance 119.

OVERSEAS CALLS

International telephone communication services are provided by Kokusai Denshin Denwa Co., Ltd. (KDD), International Telecom Japan Inc. (ITJ) and Digital Communications, Inc. (IDC). The access numbers for direct International Subscriber Dialling (ISD) calls are 001 (KDD), 0041 (ITJ) and 0061 (IDC). The rates and the areas served by these companies vary.

DIRECT DIAL CALLS

International calls can be placed directly in the same way as domestic calls. First dial either 001 for KDD, 0041 for ITJ or 0061 for IDC, then the country code, area code and telephone number. The rate is charged in 6-second units and decreases after the first minute. An economy rate with a 20 per cent discount is in effect between 7 p.m. and 11 p.m. from Monday to Friday, and from 8 a.m. to 11 p.m. on Saturdays, Sundays and holidays.

A late-night discount of 40 per cent is available between 11 p.m. and 8 a.m.

Japan has four English language newspapers: *The Japan Times, Mainichi Daily News, Daily Yomiuri* and *Asahi Evening News*; international newspapers, magazines and books are available in hotels and major bookstores.

In 1881, the English language *Japan Herald* forecast: 'Wealthy we do not at all think Japan will ever become. . .love of indolence and pleasure of the people themselves, forbid it. The Japanese are a happy race, and being content with little, are not likely to achieve much.'

MEDICAL SERVICES

Japan maintains very high standards in the medical field. There is no need to be concerned about infectious diseases or fevers. Japanese medical practitioners make full use of the most advanced techniques available in Europe and the United States, and many doctors understand either English or German. Japanese pharmaceutical products are of the highest quality. Medicines are dispensed at hospitals and clinics, where medical treatment is provided, and at drug stores, where a prescription can be filled.

There are many hospitals throughout Japan with emergency medical treatment facilities that provide a complete range of services at all times. All international hotels have emergency call-out support from bilingual doctors.

Compulsory education in Japan begins at 6 years of age and ends at 15.

Japan has no state religion. The principal religions are Buddhism, Shinto and Christianity. (For more details of these religions please see the companion series *Simple Guides to World Religions*.)

To allow a reciprocation of gifts given on St Valentine's Day (where Japanese women give presents to Japanese men), clever chocolate manufacturers invented 'White Day' to be celebrated one month later, when Japanese men are urged to buy white chocolate for their female friends. (They also give risqué presents such as lingerie.)

NOTES

Index